Amped Up
DIGITAL

Marketing Your Business from Start to Finish and Back Again

Kelly Ross Kerr

ISBN: 978-0-692-90085-7

Printed in the United States of America.

DEDICATION

To my wife Christine. Thank you for allowing me
to chase the dream for all of these years!

Special Thanks

Go to Amelia Shroyer, Brian Richardson and John Sparger.
Without your help, this book would have taken a lot longer to complete.

TABLE OF CONTENTS

Introduction

FIRST OF ALL, thank you from the bottom of my heart for picking up a copy of my book. It has been a labor of love for the past few years, and I am so excited to finally be able to share my insight and experience with you.

I have been working in the digital marketing and production industry for over 20 years. I initially started out as a web developer and digital content producer for a small start-up and eventually launched my own company, Amped Up Digital, in 2000.

I have had the great fortune of working with some amazing clients over the years. From Fortune 500 companies and "mom and pop shops" to high profile entertainers, every single one has been a fun experience and great learning opportunity.

This book will outline the process I used with my own clients to help them build and implement their marketing plans. But I don't just stick to "marketing" only; we're going to get deep. We'll work through all areas of your business from "why do you do it?" to "what is your brand?" and "are you charging enough?" to "what other products or services can you offer to create more revenue streams?" I ask the tough questions to give you the most solid plan possible

That is one of the reasons why the sub-title of this book is "Marketing Your Business from Start to Finish and Back Again". Together, we're going to work through each and every aspect of your business because "marketing" touches every corner of an organization. If the marketing doesn't work, there are no sales. If there are no sales, production can't create your product. If there is no product or service, accounting can't invoice clients. If there are no invoices, payroll can't be issued. No payroll, no employees. No employees (including you the owner), no business. Marketing is at the core of everything you do for your business. And we're going to make sure that you have a rock solid plan that puts you on the road to success.

This book and its exercises are meant to be worked through in order and repeated as needed throughout the life of your business. There are sections that will be updated as technologies and techniques change, so keep an eye on www.ampedupdigital.com for updates to the book.

There too you can sign up for the Amped Up Digital newsletter to keep up to date on future books, events, workshops, digital content and changes in the marketing industry. You'll also find a digital version of all of the exercises in the book, which can be downloaded so that you can work through them and save your progress as you go.

Again, thank you so much for spending your hard-earned money and your precious time on this book. I appreciate it more than you will ever know, and I look forward to hearing from all of you on your growth and progress. As always, if I can help you or your business in any way, please send an email to Kelly@AmpedUpDigital.com and let's have a conversation.

Kelly Ross Kerr

PART 1

REFINING YOUR MESSAGE

CHAPTER 1

DISCOVER YOUR "WHY"

O YOU WANT to know the secret to a winning marketing strategy? It's so, painfully simple. It's the "why."

Actually, it's two "whys". The first is what I like to call the "personal why."

Why are you motivated to work?

What is it that gets you out of bed every morning?

Why do you do what you do?

The personal "why" is so important because, let's face it, business is hard. There are going to be days where it feels like too much. Too much risk, too much work, too little time. The personal "why" is so critical in these moments. It keeps you focused and motivated when things get tough.

So, why do you do what you do? I'm not going to let you off the hook with cheesy, canned answers like, "because I want to make the world a better place." You need to visualize your personal "why" and make it specific. It needs to feel real, not ephemeral.

I had a client that wanted to become successful so she could buy a farm where her family could all live together. She had the entire layout mapped out in her mind down to the last detail. There were times she felt like giving up, but she could always circle back to that vision of her family farm and how it would improve the lives of people she loved. Her "why" was energy, from which she could pull, to push forward throughout the process.

In fact, your personal "why" will be relevant throughout this entire book. We identify the personal "why" so we know the motivation for our efforts. It gives us something bigger than ourselves on which to lean, and gives purpose to the second "why." The second "why" is your "product why."

Why is your product useful?

Why will people want to buy it?

Why should we care?

As the digital age rolls on, our connected lives mean that we're constantly flooded with messaging. There are ads on Facebook, suggested content on Twitter, viral news in our mailbox, marketing emails, banner ads..! We're so inundated with messaging that we, as consumers, simply won't engage with something if it doesn't capture our attention.

Now there are plenty of people who think that capturing attention is just a matter of some catchy copy with a bold font. Bright colors and punchy words can get eyeballs on your ads, but what does it take to get someone from an impression[1] to a sale? The answer is the "why."

The "why" helps you think about your product from your customer's perspective. In my philosophy, a customer is always more than a number. The more you understand your customer, the better your business will operate. Finding your "why" is absolutely crucial to determine your marketing strategy. It will literally dictate everything else you do from that point.

So how do you discover your "why?" First, think about what your product or service is and what it does. For the purpose of brevity, I'll use "product" going forward. Just know this applies to services as well. Write it down. You should be able to describe what your product is, and what it does, in 2 sentences. If it takes any longer than that, it may be too complex to explain to your target customer. What your product does is the foundation for communicating its value.

---

1. A single display of content to a user

Now you need to understand the problem you're solving. Why is this thing relevant? What does it make easier? What issue does it resolve? Why is it better than existing alternatives (if they exist)? Try to form a clear idea of what your product improves or fixes for your customer.

Determining what your product is, and what problem it solves, is the key to contextualizing your product's value to your customer. Now, one of the most important steps to discovering your "why"; identifying your customer. Who is it for? What kind of people does it help? Who would find it useful or interesting?

This is so important. You have to be able to envision your target customer. The end goal is to be able to think like them. So be as thorough as you can. Let's say your product is accounting software. Depending on the interface and features, your target audience could be solo entrepreneurs and freelancers, or it could be small business owners and agencies. It makes a difference!

Establish as much as you can about your customer group (or groups). When you've done this, you'll be able to see and order the demographics or characteristics in terms of importance. I'll give you an example from one of my previous workshops.

Paula is an entrepreneur who designed an app that would allow the user to track their pet via a GPS tracking unit attached to the pet's collar. She knew her target audience was pet owners, but it was more complex than that. When she did this exercise, her conclusion was that cat owners and dog owners, while both her target customers, needed to be separated because of the differences in dog and cat ownership.

For example, many people let their dogs outside in the backyard or off leash at a dog park frequently, whereas many cat owners keep their animals inside. Dog owners were perhaps more active or outside with their animals more often, so the connection between them and her product was more obvious. With cat owners, however, she would have to try and appeal only to the cat owners who let their cats outside on a regular basis. Otherwise, her product was only necessary if the cat got out accidentally.

It was clear that the value of her product was more readily understood for dog owners. For cat owners, her marketing strategy would have to be considered carefully. The exercise also helped her find a new target group – animal rescues. Not only could organizations that protect lost or stray animals better track animals in their care, they could also resell the tracking software to the family adopting pets from the rescue.

Paula was able to find her "why"; her product was important because people love their pets as family members. Anyone who has lost a beloved pet can relate to how painful the experience can be. Her product mattered to dog and cat owners who want to be responsible, loving pet parents.

Paula was able to push to find her product "why" because of her personal "why." Her motivation to succeed was driven by a desire to take care of her parents in their old age and declining health. She wanted to be able to hire home help so her parents could maintain their independence as long as possible and stay in their house. In the exercises at the end of this chapter, I expect you to discover both your personal and product "why."

Guided Exercises

Part 1: Refining Your Message

Exercise 1

Discover Your "Why"

In the space provided below, describe why you are driven to succeed and what you hope to accomplish personally. Be as specific as possible. This is your personal "why."

Write down a sentence or two to describe your product (what it is, what it does) in the space provided below.

Write down a problem or two that your product solves. If relevant, add in what it does better than alternatives in the market.

Write down the 3 most important characteristics of your target group (or groups) in the space below. Under these 3 characteristics, write down as much specific demographic information as possible. Use this space the way that works for you: circle things that are important, underline, draw, etc.

1. _____

2. _____

3. _____

What is your product "why" in one sentence? Write it down below:

CHAPTER 2

WHAT'S YOUR STORY?

OW THAT WE know more about your product, it's time to learn more about you. What is the main focus of your business? This is going to be crucial to figuring out your target audience and the best methods to getting out your message.

Start with your personal story. How did you get started doing the work you're doing now? Did you study it in school? Did you happen to fall into it professionally? Did you have a mentor who showed you the ropes?

Your personal story is important to understand, and it can even help build your marketing narrative. Think about how you got to be where you are, doing what you're doing. Write it down. Reflect on the steps that got you there. What hardships did you face? What moments are you proud of?

As you're thinking about all of this, I'm going to ask a really important question, and I want you to be honest when you answer.

Do you do this thing because you love it?

If you were to ask me the two most important qualities to building a successful business, I wouldn't say skill, intelligence, or even experience.

All those things are great, but they are no substitute for the two that really matter.

Are you ready? The answer might surprise you.

Passion and persistence.

The tricky thing here is that you're going to fail. Probably more than once. Starting a new business is no easy feat and there are a lot of other people trying to do the same thing. You have to be persistent so you can stick it out through the inevitable roadblocks. This is where your personal "why" comes in.

When you hit a snag, or something gets messed up, you have to keep your eye on the goal. It's easy to hit an obstacle and internalize it as a sign that you're on the wrong path. It's easy to give up. It's a lot harder to pick yourself up, dust yourself off, and come back harder and stronger than you did before.

That's why you also have to have passion. If you don't love what you're doing, how are you going to find the energy to keep at it? You have to be passionate about your work, your product, your "why" – all of it. That passion will keep you moving forward. That passion will allow you to see the silver lining when bad things happen. Passion will keep you pushing forward.

Passion also makes your work better. I know this for a fact. I had a client once, Ed, and at this step in the process, it became clear to me that he didn't have passion for his business. He was very good at it, but it wasn't what he loved to do.

We talked at length about his personal story. He had gone to school for Accounting but found that he was pretty good at coding. He fell into web development and started a business creating websites for small businesses.

The problem was, Ed really didn't like having to deal with web design. He enjoyed the actual process of coding and making something work from scratch, but hated trying to figure out how it should look. Versions of websites would go back and forth between the client and him – nit-picking over tiny design elements.

We had detailed conversations about it, but Ed kept insisting that he did love the work he was doing in his business. I decided to do a little experiment. I asked him to do two exercises.

For the first exercise, I asked him to list all the things he enjoyed doing for his business. Which tasks were exciting or challenging? What activities were done with enthusiasm rather than reluctance? Ed made this list before I told him about the other task.

For the second exercise, I asked Ed to write down all the things he might do if he had 4 more hours in the day. Let's say, somehow, a day magically became 28 hours long overnight. I challenged him to really think about what he'd spend the extra time doing. Only catch? Nothing could be related to his current business.

I've tried this exercise with many clients at this point to see whether or not they have the passion to move their business forward. With Ed, I was able to see that his passion did not lie with his current business. How did I know?

Well, for one, his list in the first exercise was extremely short. He could only come up with 3 tasks he actually enjoyed. Those tasks were coding, testing, and mentoring. Part of his business was to mentor aspiring coders who came on the team as interns. He was able to transmit his knowledge and skills to eager young people, and that was fulfilling for him. Ed also liked the active coding phase of his projects.

In the second exercise, I saw the activities for which he would use his 4 hours weren't the day-to-day, "catching up on life" kind of things you might expect from a busy, yet passionate person. No, they were things that could easily be classified as other professions:

- Start a coding program for disadvantaged youth in my community
- Build a personal finance app that helps people save more money
- Study another language
- Learn woodcarving
- Teach myself how to cook
- Develop an open source platform for people to translate their apps into other languages to open up new markets
- Take a course on robotics

As I read through this list, I knew these were things he was actually passionate about. It was clear to me that Ed would be a great teacher and had a giving and generous nature. When I showed him these two lists side-by-side, he was able to see the gap between what he loved and what he was doing.

Today, Ed is no longer building websites for small businesses. Instead, he decided to start a new business. Now he is a top-rated coding mentor. He hosts courses on different programming languages and offers one-on-one coding lessons. He now works with programmers at various levels from all around the world.

Not only is he happier doing this work, but his current business significantly outperforms his previous business. I'm convinced that it is in no small part due to the passion he feels for coding and teaching. When you love what you do, your energy is contagious.

At the end of this chapter, I'm going to give you the same assignment I gave Ed. Really think about your answers carefully – don't cheat through it because you read into my reasoning. Really allow yourself to dig deep and explore what makes you passionate. What are you willing to be persistent with?

Keep those answers in mind and reflect on what your lists tell you. Are you doing what you really love? Is your passion creating value in your business? Is there something else you'd rather be doing? Be honest, be thorough, and trust your gut.

GUIDED EXERCISES

EXERCISE 2

WHAT'S YOUR STORY?

How did you get to be where you are today? What led you to your current business? Be as detailed as possible, and include at least one hardship and one personal victory related to your business.

In the space below, write down all the tasks/activities related to your business that you truly enjoy. Think about anything particularly exciting, challenging or fulfilling.

Now, in the space below, list at least 3 different activities that you would do if you had 4 more hours in the day. These things **should not** be related to your current business.

Personal Reflection

Looking at your two lists, which list of activities do you think you would be happier doing? Which list ignites your passion and makes you feel amped up to get to work? Which list would you rather spend *the rest of your working life* doing? Be honest, and circle one:

My Business List

My Extra 4 Hours List

CHAPTER 3

FINDING YOUR AUDIENCE

NOW THAT WE'VE established what we're creating and why, we can focus on to whom we will market this product (again, or service). I cannot stress to you enough how important it is to know your audience. Part of the exercises we already worked on will help guide us through this next, very important, step.

Finding the right customer to target is like attaching the front wheel of a bicycle. You can't go anywhere without it. You need to know who they are so you can get your business off the ground. Figure out how to reach them and communicate with them. This is one of the most important exercises we will do together.

We need to know to whom we should be talking and trying to attract. Part of this comes from a deep understanding of your product and what it does. If you truly understand your product, you will be able to extrapolate who might find it valuable. Make sense?

Remember those exercises we completed in Chapter 1? I have some good news – you've already done some of the heavy lifting! From those exercises, we know (at least in part) what the problem is that we're solving for our customer. We also know a little bit about who our customer might be. Now we're going to build upon those initial insights to create our target audience.

With your exercises from Chapter 1 handy, jot down some notes about the purpose, value and problem related to your product. Looking at the demographics we already worked on, see if you can expand on that to make your group as specific as possible.

Who are these people? Where do they hang out – online or off? Do they speak a particular language/jargon? Do *you* speak that language? Where do they look for products like yours? How have your competitors reached them? Can you articulate how your product is different/better than the competition?

The more of these questions you can answer with conviction, the better you know your audience. This is so important, because knowing your audience is the first step to effectively communicating with them. So, how well do you know your target audience? My hope is, by the end of this chapter, you'll be able to say, "really, REALLY well!"

One thing I have to remind my clients of sometimes is that it's never too late to do research. You lose **nothing** by being proactive and curious. In fact, the more research you do, the better you can optimize your efforts going forward. I would encourage all savvy business-owners to constantly research, refine, and revise.

Markets are constantly changing, and the digitalization of the modern world is a huge part of that. Google periodically updates and makes changes to its search algorithms. Facebook routinely lowers the percentages of your audience who sees content on your business pages organically. New platforms come up, and old ones go away.

You have to stay on top of your brand, your audience, your niche – all of it – in order to stay relevant. So, when it comes to your target audience, you should be "checking in" with research on a regular basis. I would recommend before each campaign, and reassessing after with the campaign results and I would recommend doing some more in-depth competitor research every 3-6 months.

I know it sounds like a lot of work, but success doesn't come easily, and there is a lot of competition. You have to be willing to work hard to make sure your product gets in front of your audience in the most accessible way.

Here are some examples of research you can do that will help you better understand your target audience. We will work on these in the exercises at the end of the chapter.

- Visit your top 3 competitors on their website, social media pages, and Google them to find any recent news coverage or press releases.

    ☐ How many followers do they have on each channel?

    ☐ What kinds of content are they posting?

    ☐ Are people interacting with their content?

    ☐ Do they have coverage on any notable blogs or publications?

    ☐ What is the overall tone of their audience's comments?

    ☐ Are they responsive/engaged with their audience?

    ☐ When you searched for them on Google, was their brand website the #1 search result?

- On Twitter, Facebook, Instagram, etc., search for the name/category of your product or service (ex. "baby clothes" or "business consulting" – whatever generic term best captures your product).

    ☐ What kinds of conversations are already happening around that term?

    ☐ Are there any hashtags that seem relevant in these discussions?

    ☐ Do these conversations convey any specific problems or frustrations related to the existing products available?

    ☐ Are there any Facebook groups dedicated to communities around this product/service?

    ☐ Can you identify 10-20 "influencers" from different channels on the topic?

- Now do a Google search of the name/category of your product or service.
  - Who ranks on the first page?
  - Click on the "News" tab. Which publications are writing about it?
  - Are there any ads or sponsored search results that come up? For what company(ies)? This will give you an idea of the competition in terms of AdWords.

The answers to these questions help you with a number of things. For one, they help you identify some of your customers. People who take the time to talk about a specific product are the best kind of people. They are the ones who will engage with your brand, give you valuable feedback, and help you see potential improvements.

Especially relevant here are the influencers. These are people who have larger followings and are posting with authority on the topic related to your product. If you get an endorsement by these heavy hitters, they can refer a ton of business to you with one simple tweet/update/post.

Make a list of at least 5 hashtags that were relevant on the posts related to your product/service category. Usually, you find these more easily on Twitter and Instagram. Do the hashtags make sense for your product? Are they good "umbrella topics" for your business?

The purpose of all of this is to help you figure out exactly to whom you'll be speaking when you market your product. The better you know them, the better you'll communicate. By taking note of the kinds of conversations *already happening* in this space, you'll also have the ability to tap into those conversations **because you've done your research.**

GUIDED EXERCISES

PART 1: REFINING YOUR MESSAGE

EXERCISE 3

FINDING YOUR AUDIENCE

In the space below, brainstorm about the purpose and value of your product, as well as the problem your product solves.

Copy over the three demographics we worked on in Chapter 1. Expand this as much as possible in the space below to make your target audience as specific as you can.

1. _____

2. _____

3. _____

Research Notes: Competitors

Visit your top 3 competitors on their website, social media pages, and Google them to find any recent news coverage or press releases. Then answer the following questions in the space provided:

Write down the 3 competitor brands you will research in this section below:

1. _____ 2. _____ 3. _____

How many followers do they have on each channel?

Facebook: 1. _____2. _____3. _____

Twitter: 1. _____ 2. _____ 3. _____

Instagram: 1. _____ 2. _____ 3. _____

Google+:   1. _____ 2. _____ 3. _____

LinkedIn: 1. _____ 2. _____ 3. _____

Pinterest: 1. _____ 2. _____ 3. _____

Snapchat: 1. _____ 2. _____ 3. _____

Other: 1. _____ 2. _____ 3. _____

What kinds of content are they posting?

Are people interacting with their content? Do most of their posts have comments/shares/retweets/etc.?

Do they have coverage on any notable blogs or publications? Note them here.

What is the overall tone of their audience's comments? Is there any criticism? Take special note if they have customer complaints. It lets you know what to avoid!

Are they responsive/engaged with their audience? Do they try to resolve issues? Do they engage with people who talk to the brand?

Social Media

On Twitter, Facebook, Instagram, etc., search for the name/category of your product or service (ex. "baby clothes" or "business consulting" – whatever generic term best captures your product).

What kinds of conversations are happening already around that term?

Are there any hashtags that seem relevant in these discussions?

Do these conversations convey any specific problems or frustrations related to the existing products available?

Can you identify 10-20 "influencers" from different channels on the topic?

1. _____

2. _____

3. _____

4. _____

5. _____

6. _____

7. _____

8. _____

9. _____

10. _____

11. _____

12. _____

13. _____

14. _____

15. _____

16. _____

17. _____

18. _____

19. _____

20. _____

Make a list of 5-10 hashtags that were relevant on the posts related to your product/service category. You might find these more easily on Twitter and Instagram. Do the hashtags make sense for your product? Are they good "umbrella topics" for your business?

1. #_____

2. #_____

3. #_____

4. #_____

5. #_____

6. #_____

7. #_____

8. #_____

9. #_____

10. #_____

SEARCH

Now do a Google search (you should also do a Bing and Yahoo search, especially if your target audience is older/less tech savvy) of the name/category of your product or service.

Who ranks on the first page?

Click on the "News" tab. Which publications are writing about it?

Are there any ads or sponsored search results that come up? For what company(ies)? This will give you an idea of the competition in terms of AdWords.

Bonus Exercise

Your "Dream Customer"

A "dream customer" is someone who could radically change your business (or even your life) if they were to become your customer and/or promote your brand. Think about who this person (or persons, no more than 3) is and why their endorsement could change the game.

Who is your "dream customer" and why?

So how can you target your dream customer? I like to tell my clients to think big! Ever heard of "6 Degrees of Kevin Bacon?" The same is true here: you're very likely to know someone who knows *someone* who can connect you to your dream customer. Brainstorm the connection to your "dream customer" below and think about how you might be able to get introduced.

CHAPTER 4

WHAT'S YOUR BRAND NARRATIVE?

AT THIS POINT, you should be feeling pretty good! We know who we are as a business, we know what we're about, and we know our target audience. Now comes the creative part; how do we communicate to our audience about our brand?

Your marketing approach can be focused on the problem you're solving; it can be focused on the journey of your brand, or even what you do better than the competition. Whatever approach resonates with you the most, that's the basis of the narrative we'll craft in this section that will guide your marketing strategy.

The number one question you should be contemplating in this section is: "How do I want to portray my brand to my target audience?" This is where the research we did in the last chapter really helps us.

For one, it tells us what our competitors are doing. That will enable us to make a judgment call on whether or not *their* strategy/communication methods are working. If they are, can we emulate it or improve on it? If not, how do we avoid making the same mistakes?

Your narrative also depends a little bit on the kind of product/service you'll be marketing. If your business places you front and center, for example, if you do consulting services, then it makes more sense to tell a personal journey story. How did you get started, and how are you prepared to help clients make X better in their lives?

If your business is more product focused, then a problem-solving story might make more sense. For example, if you are selling workout equipment, your story might want to focus on the frustrations/struggles of existing equipment and how your product eliminates those problems.

Let's say both approaches make sense. For example, if you're an artist selling your work, you might want to communicate around your artistic process, what materials you use, what subjects inspire you, but also your personal story and how you got started. It is perfectly acceptable to weave more than one narrative together. We just need to be consistent.

As much as possible during this section, you should be thinking about your target audience and the research we did in Chapter 3. How might your narrative fit into the conversations already happening around your product? What kind of story might capture their attention and speak to their needs?

Look back at the articles posted about products/services like yours. What kinds of things do the articles highlight? Why do you think someone was interested enough to write an article? Can you tap into what's interesting about your product/business/journey?

Another thing to consider is on which platforms you'll be sharing your story. Are there nice images or videos that fit with the narrative you're creating? Will it be simple to create content that falls into place within your narrative? Will people *get it*?

Your marketing narrative should be consistent, but that doesn't mean it can't evolve. Once you have an idea about the story you want to tell around your brand, you can always revisit and rethink its relevance to your target customer.

Maybe your customer isn't interested in who you are; they just want the product. Or maybe they aren't so concerned about common problems within the niche. As you start to market your brand, you'll be able to draw some conclusions from how your messaging is received.

It's never too late to come back to this step and rethink your brand narrative. Remember when Netflix wanted to separate their DVD delivery service and their online streaming service into two separate brands? They wanted to call their DVD service "Qwikster," and tried to change their pricing model in late 2011.

Long story short, their customers **were not having it.** They caused such an uproar that Netflix rolled back the changes and issued an apology statement to their customers, who felt blindsided by the proposed changes. Now, Netflix is growing faster than ever. This story is important because a giant company was *willing to change course* when they wanted to do something but realized their customers didn't like it.

The key here is to think like your customer as much as possible, and then take their feedback as you test your marketing strategy. One negative comment on your YouTube video shouldn't necessarily cause you to rethink everything, but pay attention. If there's a lot of feedback coming your way that your customers want things to be different, heed their advice!

The thing about a narrative is that no one can really tell you how to do it. You're the person who knows your brand and customer best. So, ultimately, it is up to you how you want to represent your brand to the market. Be confident, be smart, and be flexible.

Guided Exercises

Part 1: Refining Your Message

Exercise 4
What's Your Brand Narrative?

In the space below, describe the key benefits your product/service provides to your customers.

If you found potential problem areas when researching your niche or your competitors, make note of them below. If not, think about what problems or frustrations might exist around your product/service.

Now write down your personal journey that led you to be interested in this niche and start your own business.

Amped Up Digital

Taking a look at the three sections you just completed, put on your "customer" hat. Which approach makes the most sense to you? Which one feels right for your brand? Which of the three do you feel the most confident discussing? Why?

Write down the three values that matter most to you in terms of your business, and briefly explain the importance of each:

1. _____

2. _____

3. _____

Reflect on these values when crafting your brand narrative. Make sure they are reflected in the story you write for your brand.

Finally, in a few sentences, write down your brand narrative. Tell the fundamental story of your product as it relates to your customer.

CHAPTER 5

SETTING YOUR BUSINESS GOALS

AT THIS POINT we're clear on what we're doing, why we're doing it, for whom we're doing it, and how we want to go about it from the big picture. Now it's time to take a hard look at where we want to go.

What's the long game? What do you want to look back on in 10 years as your proudest achievement? Where do you want to be with your business in 5, 10 or 20 years?

In this chapter we're going to talk about the "big picture" of where you want to take your business in the long term. We're also going to talk about product goals. When you're setting these goals for your business, I want you to think big and long term.

Having these goals written out and clearly articulated gives you something concrete to look at to keep you motivated and keep you accountable. We'll also lay out a timeline for you to "check-in" with yourself and measure your progress towards these goals later in the chapter.

So, how do we determine what our goals are for our business? I can't give you the answer outright, because your goals are going to be unique from anybody else's. I can help guide you to think about what I believe are the best motivations and intentions when it comes to business goals.

I actually believe there are two types of goals that every business owner should think about: the main goal and the secondary goal(s). Typically, secondary goals are either a result of achieving the main goal, or they are steps to get to the main goal.

For example, let's say you opened a restaurant. Your main goal is to get a feature in Food & Wine magazine, and your secondary goal is to maintain a 4-star or higher rating on Yelp. The Yelp rating has a more day-to-day impact on your business, but the feature in Food & Wine magazine could be a career game changer.

The feature in Food & Wine magazine is what I like to call a BHAG – Big Hairy Audacious Goal. I want you to discover your BHAG for yourself. What are you so passionate about that could change your life if you were to accomplish it? What could be the "breakout" moment of success for you and your business?

In the exercises at the end of this section, we're going to map out our BHAG and our secondary goals. What I want you to be able to do is evaluate the relationships between your secondary goals and your main goal.

Are some of your secondary goals actionable steps towards your main goal? Or do you need to first reach your main goal in order for your secondary goals to be possible? Can you think of things you can do right now to work towards your goals?

Another way I challenge my clients to think about their goals is in terms of needs. What are your most **urgent** needs for your business? What steps do you need to take right now for your business? This could be anything – from needing a website to refining your product.

Building a list of needs will help you prioritize different steps you can take to address what's lacking or unfinished in your business and marketing strategy. If any of these needs are barriers to your goals, they need to be at the top of the list in terms of what to tackle first.

Anything holding you back from working towards your goals needs to be addressed first and foremost. By putting a sense of urgency towards the goal-setting process, I try to encourage my clients to get all their loose ends tied up so they can focus on the prize.

Aside from your big picture business goals, you might have some more specific product goals or service goals. Let's say you want your product to get some sort of official certification or stamp of approval from a relevant authority in your industry.

Will that certification make a concrete difference in terms of your brand authority or your perceived product quality? Will it lead to more sales? Could it provide you with some PR opportunities?

Product and service goals should be things that will enhance your business in some way. It should give people one more reason to become a customer.

Selling an app? One of your product goals might be a high rating in the iTunes/Google Play store. Maybe you started a lawn care company. One of your service goals might be to win an Angie's List Super Service award.

Whatever it is, it should be something that signifies to your potential customers that you are a cut above the competition. It should better position you and your business for success in your given industry.

All put together, your main business goal, your secondary business goal(s), and your product/service goals will create the roadmap to get you where you want to be. In the next chapter, we're going to start building this roadmap.

Guided Exercises

Exercise 5

Setting Your Business Goals

What is your main business goal? Use the space below to describe the BHAG – the thing that could change your life and your business.

What are your secondary goals? Are they steps towards the main goal or do you need to reach it before you can tackle these?

Describe your product/service goals. Include why you think they could help your business succeed.

What do you feel are your most **urgent** needs for your business? List them below:

Are any of these needs a barrier to start working towards your goals? If so, put a star next to them.

Are there needs you could start addressing tomorrow? If so, circle them.

As we're building our roadmap in the next section, I'll ask you to come back to this list, so keep it handy.

PART 2

BUILDING YOUR ROADMAP

CHAPTER 6

WEBSITE

FTER THE GOALS are set, the next step is to dive deep into everything you'll need to do to reach them. As we build your roadmap, you should include all the individual steps and activities that will help you get closer to your goals.

We're going to create this list of "to dos", by evaluating all your marketing content and channels. Some of what we discuss in Part 2 of this book might not be relevant specifically to your business, but I'm going to be as thorough as possible to present many different possibilities for your marketing strategy.

I'm going to bombard you with questions, but you don't have to know all the answers right now. As you read these questions, take a note of anything that comes to mind, especially if it makes you think of something you're not doing that you could be doing to market your business.

I do this because I want you to discover things you haven't thought about before. I want you to understand the different potential impacts each activity could have on your audience, your brand and your business. Consider each one carefully as we move forward in building your roadmap.

The first, and most obvious, thing (to me, at least) is; do you have a website? These days, local listings and yellow pages simply aren't the way most people find the products and services they need. Instead, they're searching online. The websites that come up first are the ones they'll look at and consider.

So, first things first. Do you have a website? Are you happy with its design and content? Do you need to build a website from scratch? Do you know what platform on which you want to build and maintain your website (SquareSpace, Wordpress, Joomla, Drupal, etc.)? Does it have all the functionality you want it to have?

Do you have a domain name? Is it working for you and your audience? Is there anything you'd want to change? The domain name is going to represent your website at the highest level. Finding the right domain name can be tricky, and sometimes the one you want is already taken.

If you can get something as close as possible to your brand/company name without getting too long, you're on the right track. Think "emily-spottery.com" instead of "claypotterybyemilyjohnson.com."

Once you have a domain name, you have to build out your design and content. The way you set up your website will have an effect on how people navigate through it, and whether they stick around to learn more about your business. Having a good website is paramount.

What do I mean by a "good" website? First of all, it should look nice. It shouldn't be too cluttered and should be easy to navigate. Secondly, it should have useful content. There should be a page that clearly describes what your business is about, an easy way to contact you, and a simple to understand way to buy your products or solicit your services. Those are the basics: user-friendly and easy to navigate.

Less intuitive, but equally as important, is your content strategy for your website. Have you done sufficient keyword research to know what search terms your site should be optimized for? Do you understand how to properly optimize your pages for search traffic? Does SEO sound like Greek to you?[1]

Your content strategy absolutely needs to be optimized for the correct

---

1. To help those who want to learn how to set up their website to be optimized for search traffic on their own, but aren't sure how to go about it, I've included an SEO crash course at the end of the book.

search terms. This will be vital to not only capture organic search traffic (people who are searching with your keywords anyway), as well as paid search traffic (where you bid on those keywords to attract more clicks).

Have you looked into the average bid amount for your search terms? Have you calculated an approximate budget for paid search? Do you have a Google AdWords account? If you're just getting started, you might not be thinking about spending money on advertising just yet, but the more cohesive your search strategy, the better you can prepare your website in advance to perform well in search campaigns.

Speaking of Google, are you tracking analytics on your website with Google Analytics? Do you need help installing the tracking code to your website? Are you hitting the monthly traffic numbers you need? Are people spending time on your site, or are they leaving right away? You should be able to spend at least one hour per month taking a look at your analytics dashboard to see if you can gain any insights into how to improve your site experience.

One key metric you should always be checking is where your traffic is coming from. This is called a referral. It tells you from which site your visitor clicked to find your website. The reason why this is so valuable is because you can see which referrals are working. Maybe most of your traffic is coming from Facebook. That tells you that sharing your content on Facebook is an effective way of getting people to click over to your site. There are many other terms that are equally important, and it's important to understand what each of them mean.[2]

Do you feel confident that you can make changes, updates, and add new content to your website on your own? Are there any sections of your website that aren't complete? There's a difference between knowing you need something and doing it yourself.

If you don't feel confident tackling your search strategy alone, you should get someone qualified to help you for a reasonable price. There are a ton of platforms to connect business owners with remote freelancers who can work on digital projects. Check out Upwork, Freelancer.com and Fivrr if you need remote freelancing help.

---

2. At the end of the book, I've included a short glossary explaining the key analytics metrics, along with a brief explanation of their importance in relation to your website.

Speaking of updating your website, are you selling your products on your website? Or are you otherwise collecting leads for your services? Is your website purely informational, or can it be monetized with some kind of offering?

If you do have products, how have you priced them? Have you looked at competitor pricing? Should you be charging more? When pricing your products, it's key to make sure that your prices can be competitive without undervaluing your work.

Do you have some sort of email list-building on your website? For example, a newsletter signup, a contact form, or an emailed digital download? Are you preparing any custom content for people who sign up? Do you have a membership area on your site for custom content? Are you charging a subscription fee for such memberships?

Monetized premium content is a great option when you have the ability to regularly create a lot of content. This is good for writers, consultants, and people whose business depends on their authority as a "thought leader" in a given category. Some good examples of monetized premium content are; live webinars, video lectures, practical or insightful written content, eBooks, and printable templates.

Another good strategy for monetization is to tier subscriptions and include a free level. By offering, let's say, a digital service, for free with reduced functionality or limitations, you can get users in the door. If they fall in love with your service, they'll be more likely to pay a subscription fee to unlock enhanced features, more data, etc.

Do you have a customer service component set up to your website, such as ZenDesk? How are you planning to structure the customer service experience? Will you write out FAQs for your website? Do you have a place where people can ask questions or get in contact in case they have issues?

Many people flock straight to social media to express a bad experience with a brand. The more opportunities you give your customer to reach out to you to resolve potential issues privately, the less likely a disgruntled customer is to blast your brand on social media. Such events can be PR disasters, so it's important to have customer service strategies in place.

Speaking of social media, have you linked all your social media pages on your website? If you have shareable content (such as blog posts, images or free PDFs), have you made it easy to share on social media from your website?

Depending on your website's platform, there are various ways to enable social media sharing on specific pages, posts, or products. Social media can be one of the most powerful ways to direct traffic to your website, so you want to make it as easy as possible for people who visit your website to share your content with their networks.

All of these factors, and more, can contribute to a successful (and profitable!) website. In the exercises at the end of this chapter, you'll fill out a checklist of the things we mentioned here, and have a space to jot down any notes related to different areas. Be sure to take care to note anything you want to develop, change or add to your website.

Guided Exercises

Part 2: Building Your Roadmap

Exercise 1

WEBSITE CHECKLIST

Go through the checklist below. Check off anything you already have, and put a star next to anything you don't currently have, but would like to add. Make good use of the "Notes" section to jot down any ideas or status updates on any of the website-related items.

CHECKLIST   NOTES

- [ ] Do you have a domain name?

- [ ] Is it relatively short and easy to remember?

- [ ] Do you have a website?

- [ ] Are you happy with your website and domain name?

- [ ] Is your website easy to navigate?

- [ ] Does it have all the features you want it to have?

- [ ] Do you have help (or need help) to update/ maintain your site?

- [ ] Is your website helping you communicate your message to your audience?

- [ ] Do you have a content strategy with important keywords identified?

- [ ] Is your website SEO optimized? Do you know how to do so if not?

- [ ] Will you do (or are you interested in) paid search advertising?

- [ ] Do you (or will you) have a "members-only" area on your website?

- [ ] Are you offering custom content for members?

- ☐ Are you offering any products on your site?

- ☐ Have you priced those products appropriately?

- ☐ Have you done competitor research on pricing?

- ☐ Are you collecting email addresses to build your prospect list?

- ☐ Do you have links to your social media channels on your site?

- ☐ Do you own more than one domain name?

- ☐ If yes, are you currently using them?

- ☐ Do you have a section of your website dedicated to customer service?

- ☐ Are you currently handling customer service another way?

- ☐ Are you creating shareable content on your website?

- ☐ When you search for your domain name (without the www. and .com/org/me/etc.), are you the first search result?

- ☐ Are all of your social media pages below that in search results?

- ☐ Have you installed Google Analytics tracking on your website?

- ☐ Are you conducting a regular (at *least* monthly) analysis of the traffic your website is getting?

- ☐ Are you hitting the numbers you need to hit (in terms of monthly visitors, time spent on site, bounce rate, pageviews, etc.)?

- ☐ Do you feel comfortable with Google Analytics in terms of understanding what different stats mean?

- ☐ Do you know how to look to see where your traffic is coming from?

CHAPTER 7

CONTENT

THE CONTENT YOU provide is one of the most important parts of maintaining a successful business. It's what keeps people coming back for more. It's what provides value to anyone who might become your customer. It's what people will want to share with their networks. It's the best way for you to present yourself, your business, and your products to the consumer.

So, what kind of content are you presenting? There are many different kinds. Of course there is written content. This would include blogs, print articles, printed books, eBooks, white papers, newsletters, training materials, and workbooks.

Are you repurposing existing content? You can extend the life of your content by adapting it to various formats. For example, your printed article can become a blog article, which can be assembled into an eBook. You might also adapt some of your written content to audio or visual content.

Audio content can include recordings of presentations, coaching sessions, podcasts, live performances, audiobooks, music and spoken word.

Just like you can repurpose written content into live presentations, you can also repurpose audio content to written. Are you transcribing your audio content? Can you repurpose that into a podcast episode, an audiobook or a song? Be thinking about all the possibilities.

Are you recording video content? Perhaps you provide video coaching sessions, recorded presentations, or create a series of short videos (web series). More and more influencers are using the power of live social media video to interact with their subscribers in real time. Facebook Live and Periscope are the two biggest live video sharing platforms.

For non-live content, are you using YouTube? Vimeo? Have you integrated video onto your website? Are you part of YouTube's advertising program? Are you selling ads in your content to generate extra revenue?

Where are you distributing your audio/visual content? If you have a podcast, is it on iTunes? Libsyn? Stitcher? Soundcloud? Do you have an easy way for people to subscribe? Are you using an aggregation service? Is it monetized?

In addition to repurposing different kinds of content, are you also interviewing clients and peers or otherwise having discussions? Can you turn those into blog posts or even visual media with quotes? A growing trend on Facebook is to create simple memes with a nice image and quote text layered over.

Is there any other kind of content you can or want to create that doesn't fit into the above categories? Is there a "personal touch" you can add to your content that will make it unique in the marketplace? Are there any opportunities for you to record performances, speeches, keynotes or trainings, when you're presenting so that you can repurpose the content later?

Are there any ideas you have for products that you could create from your content? Such products could be eBooks, online training, webinars/teleseminars, web shows, films, documentaries, etc. Do you have processes or tools that you could make into a mobile or web app that your clients would pay to use? Are these things that could be "white labeled" and licensed to clients or others to use with **their clients**?

This chapter is designed to get your creative juices flowing. Think of new ways you can leverage your existing materials to create new products and/or revenue streams. If you're creating content for free, can you monetize it? If you're creating one kind of content, can you extend its life by repurposing it? Be sure to jot down any ideas you have.

Guided Exercises

Part 2: Building Your Roadmap

Exercise 2

Content Checklist

Go through the checklist below. Check off anything you already have, and put a star next to anything you don't currently have, but would like to add. Make good use of the "Notes" section to jot down any ideas or status updates on any of the website-related items.

CHECKLIST   NOTES

- ☐ Do you have a blog?

- ☐ Are you sharing white papers or eBooks?

- ☐ Is any of your written content paywalled?

- ☐ Do you (or are you able to) repurpose some of your existing written content?

- ☐ Do you own all of your content?

- ☐ Are you using some other people's material to enhance your own (music, articles, quotes, images, etc.)?

- ☐ Have you copyrighted your content or trademarked any new ideas?

- ☐ Does your content match your brand?

- ☐ Are you giving live presentations (speeches, keynotes, trainings, stage performances, etc.)?

- ☐ If so, are you recording these live presentations in some way?

- ☐ Could you develop print materials to go with them?

- ☐ Are you recording audio content?

- ☐ If so, are you having them transcribed?

- [ ] If so, are you repurposing those transcriptions into other written content?

- [ ] Are you creating video recordings of presentations, coaching sessions or trainings?

- [ ] Are you posting those videos anywhere online?

- [ ] Are you using YouTube or Vimeo?

- [ ] Are you a YouTube advertiser?

- [ ] Do you have other content ideas that haven't been mentioned?

- [ ] Can you add a "personal touch" to any of your content to separate it from competitors?

- [ ] Are you doing any online training (live or recorded)?

- [ ] If so, do you need to give certification or certificates of completion?

- [ ] Are there any products you can or would like to create from your content?

- [ ] Are there processes or tools you have developed that you could make into a web or mobile app that your clients would pay to use?

- [ ] Is any of your content relevant to your *customer's clients*?

- [ ] Could you license any of that content for third parties?

- [ ] Are you interviewing peers/customers/experts on a topic?

- [ ] If so, can you create new content out of those discussions?

- [ ] Are you selling ads in your content to generate extra revenue?

SOCIAL MEDIA

OCIAL MEDIA HAS been growing steadily for the past 10+ years, and today it is an indispensable way to reach customers. But what channels should you be present in? Is there such a thing as "too much of a good thing?" How can you tell which channels might work for your business?

A questions checklist will be at the end of this chapter, but instead of asking those questions here, I want to provide my insights into which social media channels are useful for which kinds of activities.

One thing I can tell you for sure is that almost everyone who uses social media personally considers themselves an expert in business social media. It. Is. Not. So. Yes, we are all more or less skilled at social media when it comes to representing our lives, but representing a business on social media is **another ballgame entirely**.

I can't tell you how many experienced executives I've come into contact with who have completely unrealistic goals or expectations when it comes to social media. Most companies are putting emphasis on the wrong metrics, are measuring the wrong things, are on the wrong channels, and in general aren't making the best use of the tremendous potential social media provides for deep customer engagement.

FACEBOOK

Ok, giants first. Pretty much everyone nowadays has a Facebook account, and well over 50% of active users log in *every day*. Sounds great, right? Well, it is, and it isn't.

For one, that amount of volume means incredible competition. Facebook has capitalized on that, and they have altered their algorithms significantly to favor businesses that will pay for engagement.

On average, fewer than 16% of your followers will see your page posts in their news feed. This means that, despite all your hard work to gain followers and fans on your Facebook page, unless you spend money on that post, the vast majority of your audience simply won't see it.

Not only is there a tremendous amount of content on Facebook competing for attention, but there is also the fact that Facebook's algorithms try to show people relevant content. This limits the scope of new customers you might reach.

Think about it this way: someone rides their bike to work every day. They like to race on their bike and they consume content related to bikes. Let's say you're a car sharing service. Your content won't be relevant to this bike rider, even though they potentially have need of your service.

So, organic reach on Facebook is hard. Facebook is increasingly becoming more like a paid advertising platform for businesses. If you're going to be active on Facebook, I strongly suggest you carve out a monthly budget to, at the very least, boost your posts.

Facebook is generally where people go to connect with their friends and family, play games or to share news that they care about with their networks. Many ads and business-related content can be interpreted as "interrupting" an experience that is not consumer-driven. There are a couple of ways to get around that, which I'll detail below.

One thing Facebook is great for is creating communities. The Groups feature in Facebook allows you to create open, closed, or secret (not searchable) groups, where members can interact, collaborate, and organize.

Groups are great for coaches and trainers, for example. It provides an active space for engagement and allows your customers to voice their opinions. You can also poll your group for their opinion on upcoming content, products, etc. It's a great way to get deep engagement.

Events are another useful tool for businesses on Facebook. Hosting a retreat? A coaching session? A networking happy hour? Creating an event on Facebook is the easiest way to manage RSVPs and let attendees know what to expect. Nowadays, events integrate with Google Maps, and on the mobile app, can even send a reminder to your guests when your event is coming up.

The other great Facebook tool I would recommend is something I touched upon earlier: Facebook Live. Even though only a certain percentage of your audience will see your posts in their news feed, your followers **do get a notification** when you go live. Chances are, Live posts will get more views, more interactions and more comments, because it's an interactive experience happening in real time. The best part? Those videos stay on your page for people who couldn't watch live.

If you're going to be active on Facebook, consider the tools above, and have a budget for advertising. In terms of content best practices, video and images perform significantly better than text-only content. Spice up your posts with compelling visuals or videos. Make sure your content can stand out from the crowd.

TWITTER

As someone who loves Twitter, I get a little annoyed with a lot of companies on Twitter. Twitter is a very specific kind of platform, and it is moving constantly. Because updates are so short and easy to share, you need to be on it all the time in order to stay relevant. In order to use Twitter well, you need to be light on your feet.

There are some great things about Twitter for businesses, don't get me wrong. For one, it's extremely easy to tap into existing conversations. How? Through hashtags. I mentioned keyword research earlier as being vital to your website and content strategy. Social keyword research is just as vital to your social media strategy. This is most true on Twitter, also true on Instagram, and kinda-sorta true on Facebook.

Hashtags on Twitter essentially make related content searchable. In the search field once you're logged in, any hashtag you enter will give you every single tweet that has ever used that hashtag. Twitter's search results are segmented into "Top" tweets (ie, from verified users or users with more followers or social authority) and "Live" tweets, which just means in order, with the most recent tweets at the top.

These conversations provide limitless leads, when you think about it. Any one of the tweets on that hashtag is an opportunity for you to jump in and share your thoughts or content to people who *are already interested* in the subject you're discussing. It's a great way to attract new customers and develop your position as a thought leader.

Whether Twitter will be relevant for your business or not, kind of depends on the volume of existing conversations relevant to your business. Maybe you have a very niche businesses. Twitter might only have 20-30 tweets in the hashtags you would use. Maybe those are 20-30 extremely valuable leads, or maybe it's not enough volume for you to expend your energy. You make that call – I just want to present the situation.

The thing to avoid with Twitter is anything PR sensitive. If the wrong person sees it, and they happen to have a huge following, you could be staring a PR disaster in the face. I've seen clients who are still fielding responses to a tweet that blew up even 3 or 4 years ago.

On the flip side, you need to be paying regular attention to Twitter. Sometimes there are opportunities for exposure that you need to capitalize on. Here's a great example. Last spring, Beyoncé released her single "Formation," which had a line about the seafood chain Red Lobster.

There was an incredible opportunity for Red Lobster to tweet something to acknowledge the publicity they were getting. No one was running their social media account over the weekend, so it was *days* until they finally responded. Literally hundreds of people were tweeting Red Lobster to comment about their social media inaction. Simply put, it was a lost opportunity.

In a nutshell, Twitter is a platform that can be incredibly powerful, but also potentially dangerous from a bad-PR perspective. It moves fast, and you need to pay attention to it regularly, or else you could be swept away in its current.

If you do decide to be present on Twitter, you can use third party services like Tweet Deck and Sprout Social to set up alerts for certain words or hashtags. That way, when you get mentioned, you can engage with that conversation immediately.

INSTAGRAM

Now owned by Facebook, Instagram is an increasingly popular platform upon which to share image and video content. They have now added a "Stories" feature which is shorter, live content that is only available for a limited time (it's essentially a copycat of Snapchat in that way).

Instagram tends to be a very engagement-friendly platform. People love to comment and like posts on Instagram. If you have the ability to create quality images, or if you are a public figure and people are interested in your day-to-day life or behind-the-scenes content, Instagram could be a great platform for you.

The one thing I personally don't like about Instagram is that you can't link URLs in your posts. You can have a link in your Instagram profile, but it's a lot less likely that users would click to your profile specifically to find the link mentioned in your post. So it's not great at referring traffic to your website, for example.

Like Twitter, hashtags help to link related content. As you type in the hashtag, Instagram shows you the number of posts that have used that hashtag. This is great, because you can test out different hashtags as you post, rather than having to do intensive hashtag research ahead of time.

To be successful on Instagram, you need to post regularly, include the relevant hashtags, and be consistent. Instagram is great for models, photographers, artists, public figures – essentially for creatives. If your business is super technical, it might not be the right platform for you.

LINKEDIN

You've probably used LinkedIn to look for a job or to update your resume. What you may not know is that LinkedIn has some of the best occupation-related targeting out there. So who is LinkedIn for?

People who provide corporate services, freelancers, coaches, trainers, and consultants will get the best use out of LinkedIn. Since it is a platform for professionals, those who advertise on LinkedIn can target exactly the job titles of their potential customers.

Another great thing you can use LinkedIn for is to share your written content. In addition to it being on your website, sharing content on LinkedIn will activate your professional network. If you share content in different LinkedIn groups, you will also access more people.

If your business is related to the corporate world, to small business owners or to business professionals, LinkedIn is definitely a place you should consider being present. If not, you might just want to keep it as a place to list your business, but don't put regular energy into creating posts there.

YouTube

If you have any video content whatsoever, you need to be on YouTube. Did you know that YouTube is the 2nd most popular search engine in the world? People come to YouTube every day to search for all different kinds of content.

Not only are tons of people on YouTube every day, but YouTube makes it easy to monetize your content. You can either advertise your own content, or allow your content to show other people's ads, and you'll get a small fee for each click generated from your video.

Once you become a YouTube partner, the more subscribers you have, the more potential clicks, and the higher your share of ad revenue. The partner program recognizes accounts for hitting 500,000 subscribers and 1,000,000 subscribers with a special play button that goes on their channel page.

If you're not currently doing video content, then YouTube probably isn't for you. If you have a few ideas for videos, but nothing long-term or sustainable, you still have live video options from several social media channels.

OTHERS

Other social media platforms, like Snapchat, Tumblr, Pinterest, Reddit and Foursquare are much less relevant for business and are extremely difficult to do well. Advertising on these platforms is often seen as an intrusion, in particular on Tumblr.

Snapchat is great if you are a public figure or if you like the idea of content not living forever online. Many people use Snapchat for video tutorials, cooking videos, and, of course, the filters. Snapchat could potentially be used for behind-the scenes content, but I wouldn't recommend it unless you already have a substantial following. Growing an organic audience on Snapchat is nearly impossible.

Tumblr and Reddit sort of fall into the same vein. It's threaded conversations on any number of topics. There is amazing content in both channels, but I've rarely seen such content come from a business presence. The one exception I would make is Reddit's AMA (Ask Me Anything). Professionals, celebrities, doctors, etc. have held engaging and extremely interesting live Q&A sessions on Reddit.

Pinterest is about the only channel in this section that I think businesses should consider. Pinterest has an extremely active user group, and the entire platform is designed to share and re-share content. Pinterest is great for sharing images, articles, and inspirational content.

Foursquare is relevant if you have a physical location, as it allows people to "check in" online to places they are physically in that moment. While it was much more popular several years ago, it could be relevant for your brick-and-mortar store/restaurant. If your business is strictly online, ditch it.

Guided Exercises

Part 2: Building Your Roadmap

Exercise 3
Social Media Checklist

Go through the checklist below. Check off anything you already have, and put a star next to anything you don't currently have, but would like to add. Make good use of the "Notes" section to jot down any ideas or status updates on any of the website-related items.

Checklist

NOTES

- ☐ Are you using social media?

- ☐ Are you using Facebook?

- ☐ Do you have a Facebook page?

- ☐ Do you have a vanity URL (ie. Facebook. com/businessname)?

- ☐ Are you moderating a private group for your Facebook followers/customers?

- ☐ Do you do any Facebook advertising?

- ☐ Do you have a monthly budget to allocate for Facebook ads or boosted posts?

- ☐ Are you getting adequate engagement on your posts?

- ☐ Are you on Twitter?

- ☐ Do you know which hashtags you should be tracking and engaging with on Twitter?

- ☐ Are you using Twitter ads?

- ☐ Are you using Instagram?

- ☐ Do you have a regular flow of quality images and/or video to share on Instagram?

- ☐ Are you using Instagram Stories or Snapchat?

- ☐ Are you on LinkedIn?

- ☐ Are you running any advertising on LinkedIn?

- ☐ Are you posting written content to LinkedIn?

- ☐ Are you a member of, or have you started any LinkedIn groups?

- ☐ Are you on Pinterest?

- ☐ Do you post on Tumblr?

- ☐ Are you on Reddit?

- ☐ Are you on Foursquare?

- ☐ Are you posting content to your social media channels yourself?

- ☐ Where do you get the content your post on social media?

- ☐ Do you create a monthly content calendar to keep track of your posting schedule and content?

- ☐ Are you sharing images, video, GIFs or memes with your social media content?

- ☐ Are you getting a decent amount of engagement on your various social media channels?

- ☐ Do you have a good amount of followers on each channel?

- ☐ Do you feel comfortable navigating each social media platform?

- ☐ Are you running any social media ads regularly?

- ☐ Are you on YouTube?

- ☐ Have you monetized your videos on YouTube?

- ☐ Are you part of the YouTube partner program?

EXERCISE 4
FUTURE CONTENT GOALS

Write down any future content goals you have for each of the categories below. This could be something you want to create, something you've already created that you can adapt or repurpose, or something you can turn into a product. Be as thoughtful as possible and jot down any ideas or goals as they come to you.

LIVE PRESENTATIONS

WRITTEN

AUDIO

VIDEO

OTHER

PART 3

MEASURING SUCCESS

CHAPTER 9

PIECING THE PUZZLE TOGETHER

AT THIS POINT, we've established your business goals, your brand narrative, and we've laid out your projected activities with the road map. In this chapter, we're going to tie them all together. With these pieces, one key thing we need to do is to make sure it all fits together in a way that's beneficial for your customer.

Remember those business goals we laid out in Chapter 5? We need to go through those now with the most important person in mind – your customer. Everything you do in marketing should be oriented towards creating value for your customer, so your goals should reflect that as well.

Let's say that one of your goals is to reach 100,000 followers on Twitter. That's a great goal, and Twitter accounts with follower counts that high tend to have more social authority and better engagement. But something's missing. How does a high follower count add value for your customer? This isn't a trick question – it absolutely does! Let's walk through a few examples.

For one, it gives your customer a sense of security when they research your brand. High follower counts tell your potential customer that there are enough people listening to this brand for them to pay attention.

Another thing it gives your customer is a reliable channel with which to engage with you. If you've worked hard to cultivate an audience of 100,000, you can bet that you'll be on that channel regularly, so you'll see when new mentions, followers, DMs and other engagements come in.

Remember those hashtag conversations we were going to research and keep tabs on for our social media strategy? This is another area where your goal will come in handy. If you participate in a hashtag conversation and you have a high follower count, your tweet will be in the "Top Results" tab of search results in Twitter.

This is a great thing for two reasons: one, that is the default search result view, so it's what people will see first when they search the hashtag, and two, it ensures that your contribution to the discussion stays high up in the search results, even after the tweet is several days or even months old. It gives you a sort of permanence in that hashtag discussion, so when people are looking at that, they will see your content (and be able to find your account) much more easily for a long time to come.

Getting a good spot in a popular hashtag conversation can bring you organic followers on a continual basis. It's not the only true-fire way to get engagement and grow your audience, but it is an effective one. So we know that follower counts and social media goals do have relevance for your future customers.

Now, we need to make sure that all of your goals contain the same relevance and value for your future customers. Let's think about some other kinds of goals. Maybe one of your goals is to have your website rank on the first page of Google search results for your top 3 search terms.

First of all, that's a HUGE accomplishment that will have a dramatic impact on your business, especially if those keywords are high-volume in terms of search traffic. Most people will click on the first, second or third search result, and 92% of people will click on a search result from the first page.[3]

Getting on the first page of Google search results for the most

3. "The Value of Google Positioning." *Chitika*. N.p., 7 June 2013. https://chitika.com/google-positioning-value

important keywords to your business will absolutely provide value to your customer. It tells them that your website follows the Google content rules to provide relevant and useful content for the keyword in question. It also tells your customer that you've taken the time and care to ensure that your content is top notch.

Being easy to find is one of the best things you can do for your customer. When people need a product/service, or even if they just want it *really* badly, they want to find it quickly and conveniently. For this reason, they will likely go with the first option they see that seems to fit their needs. Your goal of becoming that first option they see will enable you to better address their needs and make sure that you're outranking the competition in terms of search relevance and quality.

So some of these goals, at first glance, might not seem like they have to do with your customer at all, but if you look a little closer and think a little more in the abstract, you should be able to find the thread connecting your goals to your customer.

Lest I let you off the hook too easily, I will give you an example of some goals my previous clients tried to get away with, that did not provide value to their customers.

One guy had a personal goal to be able to afford a Porsche. When he achieved that, he started to include it into his presentation decks when he pitched to clients. It became something he showed off as a sign he could do his job well rather than offer something that benefited his customers or even helped him find more customers.

Another client had the goal of winning an award for video marketing. She was so concerned about pleasing the judges of that organization she lost focus of what would be relevant and meaningful for her customer.

Awards, accolades and personal successes are wonderful. They give us a sign that we're going in the right direction. But those forms of recognition or validation can't be our main motivation for doing what we're doing. Because that's not where the best work comes from. The best work comes from a clear understanding of, and communication with your customer.

So, at the end of this chapter, we're going to again list the goals you laid out in Chapter 5, but this time with a twist. We're also going to spell out exactly why each goal creates value for the customer, and how achieving this goal will ultimately help us better serve them.

The next piece of the puzzle after your business goals is your brand narrative. We worked on this in Chapter 4, and it should already tie well into providing value for your customer. Depending on your narrative style, that could happen in a few different ways.

If your brand is personality focused, as in, you (or possibly someone else) are the face of your brand, and your personal story tells your potential customer why you're the best at what you do. This is where you stress your background, your skills, your experience, and highlight previous successes.

For a brand narrative that is personality focused, your goals should be aligned with painting you as the best in the biz. One example of a great goal for a personality-focused brand is to get 10 excellent testimonials from previous clients.

Obviously, that will take some time and effort. You'll need to invest in your relationship-building and customer service in order to achieve that. In the end, though, it's a goal that makes sense for your business and how you communicate your brand to your customers.

Another example of a good goal for a personality-focused brand, is building up your e-mail list. Let's use the sample goal of getting to 10,000 subscribers for your newsletter. One thing this makes you do is focus on your content. If you provide the best content, you'll attract more people to sign up to hear what you have to say.

Email lists (as we've discussed in previous chapters) are great lead generation tools. Someone who loves your free content enough to sign up to receive it regularly will be a lot easier to sell to than a random person on your website. You can use email marketing like another sales channel.

Attaining that goal of 10,000 subscribers is great for your potential customer because:

a) You're creating a community of people loyal to your brand.

b) You're providing content that is valuable.

c) You're earning a position of trust with your customers.

There are some great things you can do when you have an email list that big, and the possibilities are really endless.

But what if your brand isn't about you personally? What if the products are the center focus? Goals for a product-focused brand narrative will help your product(s) stand out from the competition. One good goal for a product-focused narrative might be to get the endorsement of an influencer relevant to your industry.

Let's say you create cosmetic products that are cruelty-free. One of your goals might be to get a successful YouTube beauty blogger to review your product. When it comes to personal care items, most people want to see positive reviews or watch "unboxing" videos to get a sense of the product's quality before they buy. This is where great reviews will come in handy.

If your potential customer is researching your brand and you have great reviews, that person is more likely to buy. In a sense, all brand narratives should touch on the importance of a good reputation, but for a product-focused narrative that is especially important.

Another example of a good goal for a product-focused brand narrative is to earn an industry-relevant certification for your product/service. Let's say you're a realtor. Your service goal might be to obtain a Certified Residential Specialist (CRS) certification.

A CRS certification is widely considered to be the highest credential you can earn as a realtor. CRS designees earn almost 3x more income on average than a realtor without the certification.[4] It gives authority to your expertise as a realtor and tells your potential clients that you have invested time and energy into being the best.

Maybe you're a bit of a gourmand and you've launched a line of hot sauces. You might want to obtain an organic certificate. A "Certified Organic" or "USDA Organic" seal on your product tells your customers that your hot sauce doesn't have pesticides, chemical fertilizers, dyes, solvents, or other chemicals that more and more consumers are looking to avoid.

The important thing here is to make sure that your brand narrative fits in with your goals, and that both of these pieces also make sense in

---

4. "Designations and Certifications." *National Association of Realtors.* https://www.nar.realtor/designations-and-certifications

terms of providing value for your customer. Keep these things in mind as you look back through your goals and brand narrative that we worked on in the exercises of Chapters 4 and 5.

Last but not least, we need to consider how all your current and proposed marketing activities, laid out in your roadmap, fit into the puzzle. Looking at each activity, you should ask yourself these questions:

Will this activity help me achieve one or more of my goals?

Does this activity fit in the context of my brand narrative?

Is this activity creating value for my customer?

For every single marketing activity you include in your road map, you should be able to answer **yes** to all three of these questions. As you go through your road map, you could also start to categorize different activities as contributing to specific goals.

Segmenting your activities and tying them to your goals helps you to identify specific steps you can take to achieve a specific goal (if you opt for a "one-goal-at-a-time" kind of approach), as well as stay organized as you track your progress. The exercises at the end of this chapter are designed to help you do just that.

Guided Exercises

Exercise 1

Piecing the Puzzle Together

Have your exercises from Chapters 4 and 5 handy. We're going to start with your brand narrative. Write it down again (it's okay to make changes if you thought of revisions after reading this chapter) in the space below.

Now, let's examine the relationship between your brand narrative and your business goals. You should have primary business goals, secondary business goals, and product/service goals to consider here.

We'll include space for up to three secondary goals and product/service goals each. If you have more than that, feel free to write them out on a separate sheet of paper. In the first column, write down the goal itself. In the second, explain how the goal works with the brand narrative to create value for the customer.

PRIMARY BUSINESS GOAL   CUSTOMER VALUE

SECONDARY BUSINESS GOAL   CUSTOMER VALUE

SECONDARY BUSINESS GOAL   CUSTOMER VALUE

PRODUCT/SERVICE GOAL   CUSTOMER VALUE

PRODUCT/SERVICE GOAL   CUSTOMER VALUE

PRODUCT/SERVICE GOAL   CUSTOMER VALUE

If you had to leave anything blank in the "Customer Value" field, it could be worth reconsidering or re-working some of your business goals. Feel free to brainstorm new goals in the space below:

Now we're going to go through your roadmap. Here's how it's going to work. We're going to leave space for each of your goals (jot them down briefly), and underneath each section, list all the activities from your road map that will help you reach each goal. It's okay if some of the activities contribute to multiple goals.

The idea is to make sure that all of your activities apply to at least one goal. If they don't, think about why you want to include that activity in your marketing plan. Is it a good reason? Why or why not?

Primary Business Goal: _____
Related Road Map Activities:

-
-
-
-
-
-
-
-
-
-

Secondary Business Goal: _____
Related Road Map Activities:

-
-
-
-
-
-
-
-

Secondary Business Goal: _____

Related Road Map Activities:

- ‒
- ‒
- ‒
- ‒
- ‒
- ‒
- ‒
- ‒
- ‒

Secondary Business Goal: _____

Related Road Map Activities:

- ‒
- ‒
- ‒
- ‒
- ‒
- ‒
- ‒
- ‒
- ‒

Product/Service Goal: _____

Related Road Map Activities:

- ‒
- ‒
- ‒
- ‒
- ‒
- ‒
- ‒
- ‒

Product/Service Goal: _____

Related Road Map Activities:

- ‒
- ‒
- ‒
- ‒
- ‒
- ‒
- ‒
- ‒
- ‒
- ‒

Product/Service Goal: _____

Related Road Map Activities:

- ‒
- ‒
- ‒
- ‒
- ‒
- ‒
- ‒
- ‒
- ‒
- ‒

AMPED UP DIGITAL

CHAPTER 10

IMPLEMENTATION

CONGRATULATIONS! The hardest part of this book is over. You've established your brand narrative, your business goals, your marketing activities road map, and you've mapped out how each piece of the puzzle relates to (and depends upon!) the others. You've got a clear strategy and picture of where you want to go, and you have even laid out all the steps to get there! Well done!

This chapter is going to focus on implementation. Now that we have this awesome marketing plan for your business, how do we put it into practice in an effective way?

The key is organization. You need to be diligent when it comes to staying organized with your marketing activities. In this chapter, we'll discuss some best practices for staying organized and focused, as you implement your marketing strategy.

Since we know what kinds of activities we want to include in our marketing effort, the first step is to start doing those activities. Sounds easy, right? Unfortunately, it can get really complicated, really fast, and it's a lot for one person to handle. If you follow these best practices (and make use of some awesome organizational templates I'll share), you will be on the road to an effective marketing strategy.

First things first, you need to organize all your tools. Have you already created all the accounts you'll need? If not, you'll want to do that first. You're likely going to have an admin login for your website, a Google account login for your Analytics and/or AdWords, a listbuilding tool login (like MailChimp, ActiveCampaign, or Constant Contact), your social media logins, etc. You might also have reseller accounts on Amazon or Etsy in addition to your online store. These are just a few examples, but you get the idea.

So sign up for all of the tools you need for your marketing road map activities. It's important to keep track of your log in details for all the various tools you'll use to implement your marketing strategy. Of course, it's important for those passwords to be secure, but you need a central place where all the logistic information is stored.

One great tool for secure password management is LastPass. LastPass is a free application for secure password storage, and it also has some tools for generating really strong passwords. You can download it for your desktop or mobile phone, and store all your important logins in one place.

Now you need to make sure your website is ready to go. We talked about important elements of a good website in Chapter 6, and you should have made notes about any lingering "to-dos" you have for your website. Revisit those notes from Chapter 6 and start making any necessary changes to your website. You'll re-list these to-dos at the end of this chapter, and rank them in order of priority to help you organize those to-dos.

Before you kick your marketing strategy into high gear, you want to make sure that your website looks and feels the way you want your future customers to see and experience it. Get those features built out. Make sure all the information is clear, SEO optimized, and easy to navigate.

Again, I'll stress that if you don't feel confident making those changes yourself, *invest in your business and hire someone who can*! A bad website can absolutely prevent would-be customers from engaging with your brand. Don't risk it!

Aside from the website logistics and making sure you can access all the accounts that are relevant to your business, one of the most important organizational practices I beg you to adopt is the content calendar.

A content calendar is a document (usually a spreadsheet) that outlines all your content to be posted in a given period of time. Generally, it's built out one month at a time. If you're producing multiple kinds of content (let's say, for example a blog, social media, and YouTube videos), then you'll need multiple content calendars (or at least multiple sheets within the same spreadsheet).

Your content calendar for social media will look different from your newsletter content calendar, which will look different from your blog content calendar. However, they should be related, and complement (and promote!) each other.

You should specify somewhere in the document how frequently you'll post new content to different channels. That makes it easier to build out the appropriate amount of content. Let's take a social media calendar for example.

You might want to post to Facebook once a day, to Twitter three times per day, to LinkedIn once a week and to Instagram once every other day. Your content calendar should leave enough space under each channel so that you can build out your content appropriately for that month.

By "building out your content," I mean actually creating the updates you want to share. Write out the updates ahead of time (unless something is particularly timely and can't be planned in advance) so they will be easier to schedule. Of course, you'll want to log in to all your social media accounts regularly so you can interact with your followers, but scheduling content ahead of time can save you a TON of time and energy.

You might have 3 posts per week (on different channels) that promote a blog post; another 2-3 posts per week could share an image or a video, etc. You should develop content "categories" relevant to your business to help you keep fresh content coming.

One thing you can always share on social media is content that you don't create but that is relevant to your business somehow. We talked about this a little bit in Chapter 8, so you remember that posting content from other influencers is a great way to leverage *their* audience on your page.

If this is hard to imagine at the moment don't worry. There are templates included at the end of this chapter to help you. The most important thing about the content calendar, is that you're planning everything out in advance, so you can keep a consistent flow of new content for your audience.

A blog or newsletter content calendar might just list out the title or theme of the content in advance. Generally, we post to a blog once a week and a newsletter goes out once a month. That means the content will take longer to create, but you have more time to put it together.

A content calendar like this (for blog or newsletter) is more to keep you organized in terms of when you'll talk about different things. It's great to have this in advance to help combat the writer's block that can so often hinder our creativity!

If you'll be creating videos for YouTube or Facebook Live, maybe your content calendar will have a script, or maybe you'll just list the topics as in the blog/newsletter calendar. It depends on how you work best. Maybe you're better on the fly without a script. Maybe you're better rehearsed. Whatever works for you, make sure your content calendar is making those activities **easier and more efficient to manage**.

At this point, each activity in your road map (website, content & social media activities) should be clearly tied to your goals. For your website, you should create a to-do list for any outstanding items in order of priority, and for your content and social media, you should create content calendar templates you will use going forward.

While it might seem like a lot of work, these organizational best practices will help keep you on track with all your marketing activities. In the next chapter, we'll talk about how to measure success towards your goals when it comes to your road map.

GUIDED EXERCISES

PART 3: MEASURING SUCCESS

EXERCISE 2

IMPLEMENTATION

Look back through your notes from Chapter 6. List any "to-dos" that still need to be completed for your website. Be thorough. If you need someone to help you with any of the items you list below, put a star next to it.

☐

☐

☐

☐

☐

☐

☐

☐

☐

☐

☐

☐

☐

☐

☐

☐

☐

☐

☐

Content Calendar

In the space below, different kinds of content are listed. If you'll be creating that kind of content for your business, **circle it**. In the space below, for each content you circle, jot down **how often you want to post** new content to the relevant channel.

Social Media

- Facebook

- Twitter

- Instagram

- LinkedIn

- Google+

- Pinterest

- Other (specify below)

Blog

- Website

- Medium.com

- LinkedIn articles

- Tumblr posts

- Other (specify below)

Video

- YouTube

- Vimeo

- Facebook Live

- Other (specify below)

Audio

- Podcast

- Audiobooks

- Other (specify below)

Written Content

- White Papers

- Courses/Training

- eBooks

- Newsletter

- Other (specify below)

In the appendix of the book, you'll find a blank social media calendar template, as well as a blank template that can be used for blog, newsletter, audio, video and other written content. Feel free to adapt these content calendars for your own personal use.

CHAPTER 11

MEASURING SUCCESS

S UCCESS IS RELATIVE. How we measure our success is going to depend largely on how we work and what are our goals. Luckily, we've done some great work throughout this book to establish those goals and align them with your marketing activities.

We're going to talk about measuring success in three key areas: website, content and social media. At the end of the book, I've included some monthly reporting templates that can help you track your most important KPIs. You should, of course, fine-tune any of those templates to fit your specific goals and track the metrics that matter the most to your business.

When it comes to website metrics, Google Analytics is largely the golden standard. I've already included a Google Analytics glossary at the end of this book, which I encourage you to read through when deciding which metrics to track for your website.

It's a good idea to track Google Analytics statistics every month. By tracking your month-to-month website visits, you can gain a lot of useful knowledge. You can see if your campaigns were successful, you can see if people are spending quality time on your site, and you can see geograph-ically which places your best traffic comes from.

All of this will help you to make decisions about where you focus your efforts going forward. Let's say you notice that you have more mobile traffic than desktop. With that information, you might decide to switch to a more responsive theme that provides a better user experience for your mobile visitors. You'd definitely want to, at least, test the website on your mobile device to make sure everything flows well in the mobile experience.

If you're just getting started with Google Analytics, here are the key metrics I would recommend for beginners:

SESSIONS – the number of times a page on your website was visited

UNIQUE USERS – the unique number of people who visited your website

AVERAGE SESSION DURATION – the average amount of time someone spent on your website before exiting

PAGE VIEWS – the total number of pages that were visited in a given time period

BOUNCE RATE – the percentage of visitors who left after looking at one page and did not click anywhere else on your website (note: a low percentage is best)

PERCENTAGE NEW USERS – the percentage of visitors who are viewing your website for the first time

SOURCE/MEDIUM – viewable from your "Audience" tab, which shows you from where your website visitors came when they clicked a link to your site.

You should also track the performance of any content you publish. Sometimes, you'll use Google Analytics to track this as well. For example, you might track how much traffic your blog posts are getting on your website.

For a newsletter, you should track how many new subscribers you have with each new campaign, as well as the number of opens, clicks and unsubscribes. With certain email programs, you can even see which person on your list actually clicked on a link in your email and potentially follow up with them.

For audio and video content, some important metrics would be the numbers of views/listens, the number of likes or subscribes (to a YouTube channel, for example), shares/reposts, and comments.

On social media, it's important to track both your audience growth over time (in terms of channel or page likes/follows), as well as the performance of your individual posts when it comes to engagement. Comments and shares are a higher indicator of content value than likes, because they require more personal interaction with your content. Keep a note of what kinds of content perform best (plain copy, posts with an image, or posts with a video, etc.), and take that into account when creating future content calendars.

After a month or two of consistently tracking your performance metrics, you should have a solid idea of where you are, and be able to update or adjust your goals accordingly. Set reasonable, steady, goals for yourself and check in often to measure your progress.

These reports can be very useful if you decide to do any kind of ad partnerships or affiliate marketing. A lot of third party advertisers want to know how much traffic you're getting and what kind of audience you have. Having reports handy that show growth over time are a great way to prove the positive positioning of your website to those potential partners.

In addition to tracking month-to-month, I advise my clients to do a 6-month check-in and a 1 year check-in. For these check-ins, you'll do your reports like normal, but then also examine the progress at each 6 month level. This is an opportunity to take a deeper look at your more long-term progress, and consider how things are coming along.

Are you steadily working towards growth? Are things too stagnant? Is your strategy too segmented? Are you getting enough traffic and leads? Is your marketing success in line with your sales success? Are the two working in tandem?

During these check-ins, be open to making changes and adjusting either your goals or activities. If something you're trying isn't working, it's okay to say, "Enough of that, time to try something else." Being flexible is part of being a good business owner. Things will happen unexpectedly and we have to be able to adapt and find our stride again.

All of this is designed to set you up for success with the right perspective. You're going to be focused on the success of your company in terms of how it provides value to; and attracts customers. If you stick firm to working towards your goals, keep your activities in line with your narrative, and consistently measure your progress, your business will be unstoppable.

There's no substitute for passionate, hard work. Knowing these marketing techniques will absolutely help you achieve better success with your business, but the most important thing is diligence and consistency. Stay organized, stay positive, and amp up your business.

CHAPTER 12

FINAL WORD

THIS BOOK WAS designed with the struggles of all my previous clients in mind. It features insights they've needed, it highlights successes they've achieved, and it offers up the organizational structure that they were lacking. It has been through working with so many different kinds of business owners and entrepreneurs that I've been able to develop a clear picture of what works – no matter what industry you're in.

What I see, time and time again, is that it comes down to what your motivations are. Your heart has to be in it. You have to have goals that keep you motivated and energized. You can't get lazy and you can't get discouraged.

One of my oldest clients didn't get started with her business until she was 65. She had worked as a teacher for most of her adult life, and she wanted to retire with some steady income by starting a side business selling handmade crafts on Etsy and Amazon.

When she started, she had no marketing strategy to speak of, but she had the Etsy store set up and several products available to sell. When I got her to activate her social media activities, she started getting a ton of orders. Turns out, being a beloved teacher means a lot of former students are willing to support you. They shared her page with hundreds of their friends and she has seen steady growth ever since.

In her case, it was a matter of putting herself out there. For you, it might be something else that you have to overcome or see from a different perspective to correct. My point is that throughout the times when things might not be going great, you stay focused and dedicated to your business.

It is my sincere hope that the advice and strategies covered in this book are able to make the difference between a side job and a successful, independent business. Everyone deserves the chance to make their dreams come true, especially you!

APPENDIX

SEO Crash Course

1. Keywords

    a. Keywords are important because it's how people searching online will find your business. They should be as close as possible to your product or service (they should be relevant, in other words).

    b. Your keywords should have reasonably high search volume. You want to be using terms that people are actually searching for. You can use Google's Keyword Planner tool from your AdWords account to do a search of keywords to find out how much traffic those terms get in a given month.

    c. You should have one "focus keyword" specific to each page of your website. This means including that keyword in your meta data, in your headers, and within the body of text on your page

2. Meta Data

    a. Meta data is the title of your page and the description of your page. Both have character limits, and both show up together in search results. Your page title is also visible at the top of the browser or tab.

b. Your meta title should be 55-60 characters (no more than 60), and your meta description should be 150-160 characters (no more than 160).

c. Search websites like Google and Bing use scanning robots, called crawlers, to look for terms contained in your meta data to categorize search results. Essentially, they are scanning for terms that correlate to what someone is searching for at any given time.

d. Meta data factors into how high up on the search results page your website might rank for any given keyword.

e. Meta data is also the primary content that anyone searching for products and services like yours might see. Your title and description should make sense, and be compelling enough to click on.

3. Headers

a. In addition to meta data, crawlers also scan individual web pages for keywords in headers. Headers signify to crawlers what is the most important content on the page. Think about them as the chapter titles in a book. They help to tell search engines what your content is about.

b. Your most important keywords should be a part of your headers. Headers are ranked in terms of importance from H1 to H6. Most crawlers only care about H1, H2 and H3.

c. A header that is tagged H1 is your most important header on the page. It should contain the main keyword you want the page to rank for, if possible. An H2 header is your sub-header, and can contain your focus keyword or terms relevant to it. An H3 header is related to your H2 tag, but less important.

d. Here's an example for a page selling shoes:

- H1: Shoes for Men and Women
- H2: Women's Boots, Heels, Sandals & Flats

- H3: Men's Dress Shoes, Loafers and Sneakers
- The most important content is that the page has shoes for men and women. Women's shoes happen to sell more for this retailer, so the H2 tag highlights women's shoe terms. H3 covers the offerings for men.

As you build out the content for each page of your website, you should have:

- A focus keyword for each page
- A meta title of 50-60 characters containing your focus keyword
  - Ex: Pet Products for Dogs, Cats, Birds & Fish – Sara's Pet Store
    - Find quality pet products including pet food, toys, cleaning products and carriers for dogs, cats, birds & fish at Sara's Pet Store in downtown Cincinnati.
- H1, H2, and H3 within the text of your page containing your most important keywords.

Google Analytics

Audience Overview (default dashboard)

The Audience Overview is the default dashboard that appears when you click on your website from the Google Analytics page. It gives you a brief overview of key metrics for a given time period. Adjust the time period to the desired time in the top right corner. Generally, monthly statistics are best.

Sessions

Sessions are the total number of times your site was visited. This could include multiple visits from the same user.

Users

The unique number of users that visited your website. These are the individual people who clicked on your site. This number is generally a bit lower than "sessions" because sometimes people visit the website more than once in a given time frame.

PAGEVIEWS

This is the number of pages on your site that were viewed. This number should also be higher than the number of sessions and users. It means that each user (or each session) visited multiple pages. That's good – we want people to click through to different pages on our site.

PAGES/SESSION

Pages/Session is the average number of pages that someone visited in a session. The higher this number, the more people are exploring your different content when they access the site.

AVERAGE SESSION DURATION

This is the average amount of time a user is spending on your site each time they visit your website (initiate a session). It is presented in hours:minutes:seconds. A good session duration is higher than one minute. The longer your users stay on your site, the more relevant and interesting your website and content.

BOUNCE RATE

This is the percentage of users who, after entering your website on a given page, left the site (closed the tab or browser window) without visiting any other pages. You want to keep your bounce rate as low as possible (by keeping people interested in different pages on your site). A bounce rate of 75% or higher is widely considered bad. Sometimes, paid campaigns will cause your bounce rate to increase. Try to keep it as low as possible.

% NEW SESSIONS

This is the percentage of users who have never previously visited your site. This can be good or bad – it depends upon your website goals. Do you want to have a core group of customers who are extremely loyal and keep coming back? Then a low percentage of new sessions is probably fine – it means that people are coming back over time for more.

If, however, you want to be attracting new customers, you might prefer to have a higher percentage of new sessions month-to-month. In any case, it gives you an idea of your "brand loyalty" in terms of your website. Are people visiting once and then leaving? Are they coming back time and time again? Consider any recent changes to your website when you think about this metric. Did you add content that brought people back? Did you start a campaign that got a lot of new people to visit your site?

ACQUISITION

The acquisition section of Google Analytics allows us to see where people are coming from when they visit our site. This is very useful to help you focus in on things that are working, or perhaps stop an activity that isn't bringing people to your site.

OVERVIEW

In the overview dashboard, you can see the top channels of traffic (from where the traffic originates), the number of sessions graphed according to the dates being displayed (you can change the dates in the top right), and a general look at different metrics we discussed above as it relates to each channel.

DIRECT TRAFFIC means that someone opened their browser and typed your website name specifically in order to access your site. They didn't click on anything, they just knew about your site and visited it directly.

SOCIAL TRAFFIC means any traffic that was clicked on from social media platforms, including Facebook, Twitter, Google+, LinkedIn, Instagram, etc. This is valuable for you to see which social media platforms give you the highest number of visits (we'll dive into this a little deeper in "Source/Medium").

REFERRAL TRAFFIC means any other websites that have your website linked on them. This includes blogs, directories, news articles, etc. Referrals also create backlinks for your site, which helps your search rankings. The more external websites that link to yours, the more authority Google will assign to your website, and the higher up you will appear in search results.

ORGANIC SEARCH means that someone was searching for something and found your website organically. Typically, this happens because you have a good SEO strategy implemented on your website. Organic search traffic is great, and it's a good indication that your website is performing well according to Google's standards.

PAID SEARCH is, of course, any traffic that was a result of your AdWords campaigns. These are visits that were initiated because someone clicked on your ad or your promoted search result.

There are a few other channels, but they aren't common. They include Email, Affiliates, Other Advertising, and Display. You can learn more about these terms at https://support.google.com/analytics/answer/3297892.

All Traffic
- Channels
A deeper look at the metrics per channel. From this view, you can click on any of the channels to see specific metrics for those sessions.

- Treemaps
Treemaps are an advanced feature of analytics that helps you explore trends in your acquisitions. It is supposed to help you draw conclusions about your oncoming traffic.

- Source/Medium
Source/Medium is similar to channels, but it is more specific. Instead of seeing "social," for example, you'll see "facebook.com" along with other social media channels. You'll see the individual domains that linked to you instead of "referral." It's more specific information about where your traffic is coming from.

This is so important because it can help you see which efforts on your end are working. For example, if you started to post more on Facebook, and you see a sharp increase in Facebook traffic, you'll know to continue or expand upon your Facebook activities.

- Referrals
The referrals view is extremely similar to Source/Medium, however,

Source/Medium is more accurate. Why? Because of something called UTM parameters. Most skilled marketers include UTM parameters in any of their campaign links.

UTM parameters contain campaign data to help you track a source, medium, and campaign name. If there are UTM parameters in the URL, Google Analytics will show you that visit in the Source/Medium instead of Referral, and that traffic won't be in the Referral reports.

BEHAVIOR

Simply put, Behavior tells you how the users have behaved on your website. What pages did they visit? What are your most popular pages? Which blog post didn't perform well? Viewing the stats under Behavior will give you valuable information about the relevancy of your content.

SITE CONTENT – ALL PAGES

Remember the metrics we defined at the beginning of this glossary? In Site Content – All Pages, you get to see the average of each of those metrics for *individual pages* on your website. This helps you to see which pages are super relevant because people are spending time on them (average session duration).

Consider all of these statistics to evaluate the effectiveness of your content. Do some of your pages have a ton more views than others? Are some of your pages experiencing lots of time on the site, versus others where people leave after a few seconds? Is the bounce rate very different between the different pages? Use this view to draw conclusions about your content.

Content Calendars

Social Media

Channel	Date	Time	Copy	Character Count

Blog/Newsletter

Blog Date	Time	Title	Excerpt	Meta Title